Gratitude Journal

90 Days Of Gratitude Journaling

Name: ◇◇◇◇◇◇◇◇◇◇◇◇◇◇◇◇◇◇◇◇◇◇◇◇◇◇◇◇◇◇◇◇◇◇◇◇

Email: ◇◇◇◇◇◇◇◇◇◇◇◇◇◇◇◇◇◇◇◇◇◇◇◇◇◇◇◇◇◇◇◇◇◇◇◇

Copyright © 2020 Ericka Williams. All rights reserved.
Published by SW Investments TX LLC
ISBN 978-1-7342082-1-4

All rights reserved, including the right to reproduce this book or portions thereof in any form whatsoever. For information, address the publisher.

All rights reserved. This book or parts thereof may not be reproduced in any form, stored in any retrieval system, or transmitted in any form by any means—electronic, mechanical, photocopy, recording, or otherwise—without prior written permission of the publisher, except as provided by United States of America copyright law. For permission requests, write to the publisher, at "Attention: Permissions Coordinator," at the address below:
Ericka.s.williams@gmail.com

LET'S MAKE GRATITUDE A HABIT

As you write in your journal check off the boxes to celebrate your consistency.

WEEK

	M	T	W	T	F	S	S
1	☐	☐	☐	☐	☐	☐	☐
2	☐	☐	☐	☐	☐	☐	☐
3	☐	☐	☐	☐	☐	☐	☐
4	☐	☐	☐	☐	☐	☐	☐
5	☐	☐	☐	☐	☐	☐	☐
6	☐	☐	☐	☐	☐	☐	☐
7	☐	☐	☐	☐	☐	☐	☐
8	☐	☐	☐	☐	☐	☐	☐
9	☐	☐	☐	☐	☐	☐	☐
10	☐	☐	☐	☐	☐	☐	☐
11	☐	☐	☐	☐	☐	☐	☐
12	☐	☐	☐	☐	☐	☐	☐

Thank you so much for purchasing this gratitude journal. Gratitude has drastically improved my life in my ways. According to a Harvard health article. "Gratitude is strongly and consistently associated with greater happiness. Gratitude helps people feel more positive emotions, relish good experiences, improve their health, deal with adversity, and build strong relationships."

We'd love for you to write in this every day, but we know that's hard but in order to achieve a long term goal you need to write in it daily, it will help you attitude.

You should plan to write in this gratitude journal for 15 minutes before you go to bed, set an alarm on your phone, or put a reminder in your calendar. I found it easier to write at night for me because then I get to think about my day.

—*Ericka Williams*

DAILY *Gratitude*

DATE : ____ ____ ____

◇◇

I am grateful for...

_____
_____
_____
_____

Today I'm proud that I...

_____
_____
_____

How do you feel today?:

- ☐ Happy
- ☐ Sad
- ☐ Stressed
- ☐ Energized
- ☐ Tired
- ☐ Stressed
- ☐ Fearful
- ☐ Angry

- ☐ Peaceful
- ☐ Disappointed
- ☐ Anxious
- ☐ Annoyed
- ☐ Hopeful
- ☐ Calm
- ☐ Productive
- ☐ Excited

- ☐ Negative
- ☐ Strong
- ☐ Inspired
- ☐ Thankful
- ☐ Loving
- ☐ Loved
- ☐ _____
- ☐ _____

_____
_____

What did you become more self aware of this year?

_____
_____
_____
_____
_____
_____
_____

DAILY
Gratitude

DATE : ____ ____ ____

∞∞

I am grateful for...
_____
_____
_____
_____

What are you taking for granted about your day to day that you could be thankful for?
_____
_____
_____
_____
_____
_____

How do you feel today?:

- ☐ Happy
- ☐ Sad
- ☐ Stressed
- ☐ Energized
- ☐ Tired
- ☐ Stressed
- ☐ Fearful
- ☐ Angry

- ☐ Peaceful
- ☐ Disappointed
- ☐ Anxious
- ☐ Annoyed
- ☐ Hopeful
- ☐ Calm
- ☐ Productive
- ☐ Excited

- ☐ Negative
- ☐ Strong
- ☐ Inspired
- ☐ Thankful
- ☐ Loving
- ☐ Loved
- ☐ _____
- ☐ _____

_____
_____

> Take Action: Write an email to someone who has positively impacted your life

☐ Task Completed

DAILY *Gratitude*

DATE : ____ ____ ____

I am grateful for...

_____
_____
_____
_____
_____

Positive Affirmation: I am...

_____
_____
_____

How do you feel today?:

- ☐ Happy
- ☐ Sad
- ☐ Stressed
- ☐ Energized
- ☐ Tired
- ☐ Stressed
- ☐ Fearful
- ☐ Angry

- ☐ Peaceful
- ☐ Disappointed
- ☐ Anxious
- ☐ Annoyed
- ☐ Hopeful
- ☐ Calm
- ☐ Productive
- ☐ Excited

- ☐ Negative
- ☐ Strong
- ☐ Inspired
- ☐ Thankful
- ☐ Loving
- ☐ Loved
- ☐ _____
- ☐ _____

_____
_____

List 5 body parts you're thankful for and why?

1. _____
2. _____
3. _____
4. _____
5. _____

DAILY
Gratitude

DATE : ____ ____ ____

I am grateful for...
_____
_____
_____
_____

What's something that you just accomplished? How do you feel about it can be big or small.
_____
_____
_____
_____
_____
_____

How do you feel today?:

- ☐ Happy
- ☐ Sad
- ☐ Stressed
- ☐ Energized
- ☐ Tired
- ☐ Stressed
- ☐ Fearful
- ☐ Angry

- ☐ Peaceful
- ☐ Disappointed
- ☐ Anxious
- ☐ Annoyed
- ☐ Hopeful
- ☐ Calm
- ☐ Productive
- ☐ Excited

- ☐ Negative
- ☐ Strong
- ☐ Inspired
- ☐ Thankful
- ☐ Loving
- ☐ Loved
- ☐ _____
- ☐ _____

I could have made today better by:
_____
_____
_____
_____

DAILY
Gratitude

DATE : ____ ____ ____

◇◇

I am grateful for...

_____
_____
_____
_____

Today I'm proud that I...

_____
_____
_____

How do you feel today?:

- ☐ Happy
- ☐ Sad
- ☐ Stressed
- ☐ Energized
- ☐ Tired
- ☐ Stressed
- ☐ Fearful
- ☐ Angry

- ☐ Peaceful
- ☐ Disappointed
- ☐ Anxious
- ☐ Annoyed
- ☐ Hopeful
- ☐ Calm
- ☐ Productive
- ☐ Excited

- ☐ Negative
- ☐ Strong
- ☐ Inspired
- ☐ Thankful
- ☐ Loving
- ☐ Loved
- ☐ _____
- ☐ _____

_____
_____

What are somethings you need to focus on that matter?

_____
_____
_____
_____
_____
_____
_____

DAILY
Gratitude

DATE : ____ ____ ____

◇◇

I am grateful for...
_____
_____
_____
_____

On days when I'm feeling blue, what is something I can do?
_____
_____
_____
_____
_____
_____
_____

How do you feel today?:

☐ Happy	☐ Peaceful	☐ Negative
☐ Sad	☐ Disappointed	☐ Strong
☐ Stressed	☐ Anxious	☐ Inspired
☐ Energized	☐ Annoyed	☐ Thankful
☐ Tired	☐ Hopeful	☐ Loving
☐ Stressed	☐ Calm	☐ Loved
☐ Fearful	☐ Productive	☐ _____
☐ Angry	☐ Excited	☐ _____

Notes:
_____
_____
_____
_____

DAILY
Gratitude

DATE : ____ ____ ____

"Don't judge your feelings; notice them. Use them as your map. Don't be afraid of the truth." – Lori Gottlieb

I am grateful for...
_____
_____
_____

Am I holding on to something I need to let go of?
_____
_____
_____

How do you feel today?:

- ☐ Happy
- ☐ Sad
- ☐ Stressed
- ☐ Energized
- ☐ Tired
- ☐ Stressed
- ☐ Fearful
- ☐ Angry

- ☐ Peaceful
- ☐ Disappointed
- ☐ Anxious
- ☐ Annoyed
- ☐ Hopeful
- ☐ Calm
- ☐ Productive
- ☐ Excited

- ☐ Negative
- ☐ Strong
- ☐ Inspired
- ☐ Thankful
- ☐ Loving
- ☐ Loved
- ☐ _____
- ☐ _____

_____
_____

Who are some people you haven't talk to in awhile that make you happy that you'd like to call?
_____
_____
_____
_____
_____

DAILY
Gratitude

DATE : ____ ____ ____

I am grateful for...

_____
_____
_____
_____

Make a list of 15 things that make you smile

- _____
- _____
- _____
- _____
- _____
- _____
- _____
- _____
- _____
- _____
- _____
- _____
- _____
- _____
- _____

The words I'd like to live by are:

_____
_____
_____
_____
_____
_____
_____

DAILY
Gratitude

DATE : ____ ____ ____

I am grateful for...
_____
_____
_____
_____
_____

Today I'm proud that I...
_____
_____
_____
_____

How do you feel today?:

- ☐ Happy
- ☐ Sad
- ☐ Stressed
- ☐ Energized
- ☐ Tired
- ☐ Stressed
- ☐ Fearful
- ☐ Angry

- ☐ Peaceful
- ☐ Disappointed
- ☐ Anxious
- ☐ Annoyed
- ☐ Hopeful
- ☐ Calm
- ☐ Productive
- ☐ Excited

- ☐ Negative
- ☐ Strong
- ☐ Inspired
- ☐ Thankful
- ☐ Loving
- ☐ Loved
- ☐ _____
- ☐ _____

_____
_____

What do you miss about seeing people daily?
_____
_____
_____
_____
_____
_____
_____

DAILY
Gratitude

DATE : _____ _____ _____

I am grateful for...
_____
_____
_____
_____

Write about the music you're thankful for to be able to listen to and why?
_____
_____
_____
_____
_____
_____

How do you feel today?:

- ☐ Happy
- ☐ Sad
- ☐ Stressed
- ☐ Energized
- ☐ Tired
- ☐ Stressed
- ☐ Fearful
- ☐ Angry

- ☐ Peaceful
- ☐ Disappointed
- ☐ Anxious
- ☐ Annoyed
- ☐ Hopeful
- ☐ Calm
- ☐ Productive
- ☐ Excited

- ☐ Negative
- ☐ Strong
- ☐ Inspired
- ☐ Thankful
- ☐ Loving
- ☐ Loved
- ☐ _____
- ☐ _____

_____
_____

⊙ Take Action: Text someone that you were thinking about today.

☐ Seriously, Send the text.

DAILY
Gratitude

DATE : ____ ____ ____

I am grateful for...
_____
_____
_____
_____

Positive Affirmation: I am...
_____
_____
_____

How do you feel today?:

- ☐ Happy
- ☐ Sad
- ☐ Stressed
- ☐ Energized
- ☐ Tired
- ☐ Stressed
- ☐ Fearful
- ☐ Angry

- ☐ Peaceful
- ☐ Disappointed
- ☐ Anxious
- ☐ Annoyed
- ☐ Hopeful
- ☐ Calm
- ☐ Productive
- ☐ Excited

- ☐ Negative
- ☐ Strong
- ☐ Inspired
- ☐ Thankful
- ☐ Loving
- ☐ Loved
- ☐ _____
- ☐ _____

_____
_____

List 5 body parts you're thankful for and why?
1. _____
2. _____
3. _____
4. _____
5. _____

DAILY
Gratitude

DATE : ____ ____ ____

◇◇

I am grateful for...

_____
_____
_____
_____

What do you love most about yourself?

_____
_____
_____
_____
_____
_____

How do you feel today?:

- ☐ Happy
- ☐ Sad
- ☐ Stressed
- ☐ Energized
- ☐ Tired
- ☐ Stressed
- ☐ Fearful
- ☐ Angry

- ☐ Peaceful
- ☐ Disappointed
- ☐ Anxious
- ☐ Annoyed
- ☐ Hopeful
- ☐ Calm
- ☐ Productive
- ☐ Excited

- ☐ Negative
- ☐ Strong
- ☐ Inspired
- ☐ Thankful
- ☐ Loving
- ☐ Loved
- ☐ _____
- ☐ _____

I could have made today better by:

_____
_____
_____

DAILY
Gratitude

DATE : ____ ____ ____

I am grateful for...
___
___
___
___

Today I'm proud that I...
___
___
___

How do you feel today?:

- ☐ Happy
- ☐ Sad
- ☐ Stressed
- ☐ Energized
- ☐ Tired
- ☐ Stressed
- ☐ Fearful
- ☐ Angry

- ☐ Peaceful
- ☐ Disappointed
- ☐ Anxious
- ☐ Annoyed
- ☐ Hopeful
- ☐ Calm
- ☐ Productive
- ☐ Excited

- ☐ Negative
- ☐ Strong
- ☐ Inspired
- ☐ Thankful
- ☐ Loving
- ☐ Loved
- ☐ _____
- ☐ _____

___
___

How have you grown this past year?
___
___
___
___
___
___
___

DAILY
Gratitude

DATE : ____ ____ ____

I am grateful for...
_____
_____
_____
_____

What do you want to improve upon most next year?
_____
_____
_____
_____
_____
_____
_____
_____
_____

How do you feel today?:

- ☐ Happy
- ☐ Sad
- ☐ Stressed
- ☐ Energized
- ☐ Tired
- ☐ Stressed
- ☐ Fearful
- ☐ Angry

- ☐ Peaceful
- ☐ Disappointed
- ☐ Anxious
- ☐ Annoyed
- ☐ Hopeful
- ☐ Calm
- ☐ Productive
- ☐ Excited

- ☐ Negative
- ☐ Strong
- ☐ Inspired
- ☐ Thankful
- ☐ Loving
- ☐ Loved
- ☐ _____
- ☐ _____

DAILY
Gratitude

DATE : ____ ____ ____

◇◇

"Everything negative — pressure, challenges — is all an opportunity for me to rise." — Kobe Bryant

I am grateful for...
_____
_____
_____

Am I holding on to something I need to let go of?
_____
_____
_____

How do you feel today?:

☐ Happy	☐ Peaceful	☐ Negative
☐ Sad	☐ Disappointed	☐ Strong
☐ Stressed	☐ Anxious	☐ Inspired
☐ Energized	☐ Annoyed	☐ Thankful
☐ Tired	☐ Hopeful	☐ Loving
☐ Stressed	☐ Calm	☐ Loved
☐ Fearful	☐ Productive	☐ _____
☐ Angry	☐ Excited	☐ _____

_____

What activates and hobbies would you miss if you weren't able to do them?
_____
_____
_____
_____
_____
_____

DAILY
Gratitude

DATE : ____ ____ ____

I am grateful for...

What is your favorite activity that you do just for yourself? Have you done it lately?

What is your biggest motivation for success?

DAILY
Gratitude

DATE : ____ ____ ____

I am grateful for...
_____
_____
_____
_____

Today I'm proud that I...
_____
_____
_____

How do you feel today?:

- ☐ Happy
- ☐ Sad
- ☐ Stressed
- ☐ Energized
- ☐ Tired
- ☐ Stressed
- ☐ Fearful
- ☐ Angry

- ☐ Peaceful
- ☐ Disappointed
- ☐ Anxious
- ☐ Annoyed
- ☐ Hopeful
- ☐ Calm
- ☐ Productive
- ☐ Excited

- ☐ Negative
- ☐ Strong
- ☐ Inspired
- ☐ Thankful
- ☐ Loving
- ☐ Loved
- ☐ _____
- ☐ _____

What was the most important lesson your mother taught you?
_____
_____
_____
_____
_____
_____
_____

DAILY
Gratitude

DATE : ____ ____ ____

◇◇

I am grateful for...

_____
_____
_____
_____

What was the most important lesson your father taught you?

_____
_____
_____
_____
_____
_____

How do you feel today?:

- ☐ Happy
- ☐ Sad
- ☐ Stressed
- ☐ Energized
- ☐ Tired
- ☐ Stressed
- ☐ Fearful
- ☐ Angry

- ☐ Peaceful
- ☐ Disappointed
- ☐ Anxious
- ☐ Annoyed
- ☐ Hopeful
- ☐ Calm
- ☐ Productive
- ☐ Excited

- ☐ Negative
- ☐ Strong
- ☐ Inspired
- ☐ Thankful
- ☐ Loving
- ☐ Loved
- ☐ _____
- ☐ _____

_____
_____

> Take Action: Send an amazon gift card to a friend or family member that's far away.

☐ Completed

DAILY
Gratitude

DATE : ____ ____ ____

◇◇◇

I am grateful for...

_____
_____
_____
_____

Positive Affirmation: I am...

_____
_____
_____

How do you feel today?:

☐ Happy   ☐ Peaceful   ☐ Negative
☐ Sad   ☐ Disappointed   ☐ Strong
☐ Stressed   ☐ Anxious   ☐ Inspired
☐ Energized   ☐ Annoyed   ☐ Thankful
☐ Tired   ☐ Hopeful   ☐ Loving
☐ Stressed   ☐ Calm   ☐ Loved
☐ Fearful   ☐ Productive   ☐ _____
☐ Angry   ☐ Excited   ☐ _____

_____
_____

What aspects of your work environment are you thankful for?
_____
_____
_____
_____
_____
_____
_____

DAILY
Gratitude

DATE : ____ ____ ____

◊◊

I am grateful for...

_____
_____
_____
_____

What are your 3 biggest strengths?

_____
_____
_____
_____
_____
_____

How do you feel today?:

- ☐ Happy
- ☐ Sad
- ☐ Stressed
- ☐ Energized
- ☐ Tired
- ☐ Stressed
- ☐ Fearful
- ☐ Angry

- ☐ Peaceful
- ☐ Disappointed
- ☐ Anxious
- ☐ Annoyed
- ☐ Hopeful
- ☐ Calm
- ☐ Productive
- ☐ Excited

- ☐ Negative
- ☐ Strong
- ☐ Inspired
- ☐ Thankful
- ☐ Loving
- ☐ Loved
- ☐ _____
- ☐ _____

I could have made today better by:

_____
_____
_____
_____

DAILY
Gratitude

DATE : _____ _____ _____

I am grateful for...

_____
_____
_____
_____

Today I'm proud that I...

_____
_____
_____
_____

How do you feel today?:

- ☐ Happy
- ☐ Sad
- ☐ Stressed
- ☐ Energized
- ☐ Tired
- ☐ Stressed
- ☐ Fearful
- ☐ Angry

- ☐ Peaceful
- ☐ Disappointed
- ☐ Anxious
- ☐ Annoyed
- ☐ Hopeful
- ☐ Calm
- ☐ Productive
- ☐ Excited

- ☐ Negative
- ☐ Strong
- ☐ Inspired
- ☐ Thankful
- ☐ Loving
- ☐ Loved
- ☐ _____
- ☐ _____

What's the most important lesson that life has taught you this year?

_____
_____
_____
_____
_____
_____

DAILY
Gratitude

DATE : ____ ____ ____

◇◇

I am grateful for...

_____
_____
_____
_____

What's a hard lesson that you were grateful to learn?

_____
_____
_____
_____
_____
_____
_____
_____
_____

How do you feel today?:

☐ Happy	☐ Peaceful	☐ Negative
☐ Sad	☐ Disappointed	☐ Strong
☐ Stressed	☐ Anxious	☐ Inspired
☐ Energized	☐ Annoyed	☐ Thankful
☐ Tired	☐ Hopeful	☐ Loving
☐ Stressed	☐ Calm	☐ Loved
☐ Fearful	☐ Productive	☐ _____
☐ Angry	☐ Excited	☐ _____

DAILY
Gratitude

DATE : ____ ____ ____

"When we do the best we can, we never know what miracle is wrought in our life or the life of another." — Helen Keller

I am grateful for...
_____
_____
_____

What's one thoughtful thing someone did for you recently?
_____
_____
_____

How do you feel today?:

☐ Happy	☐ Peaceful	☐ Negative
☐ Sad	☐ Disappointed	☐ Strong
☐ Stressed	☐ Anxious	☐ Inspired
☐ Energized	☐ Annoyed	☐ Thankful
☐ Tired	☐ Hopeful	☐ Loving
☐ Stressed	☐ Calm	☐ Loved
☐ Fearful	☐ Productive	☐ _____
☐ Angry	☐ Excited	☐ _____

_____
_____

Have you had a chance to help someone recently, and how did that make you feel?
_____
_____
_____
_____
_____
_____

DAILY
Gratitude

DATE : ____ ____ ___

∞∞

I am grateful for...
_____
_____
_____
_____

List 3 things that went well for you this week?
Next to each also answer why it went well?
_____
_____
_____
_____
_____
_____
_____
_____
_____
_____
_____
_____
_____
_____

Who is a teacher or mentor that has made an impact on your life and how did they help you?
_____
_____
_____
_____
_____
_____
_____

DAILY
Gratitude

DATE : ____ ____ ____

I am grateful for...
_____
_____
_____
_____

Today I'm proud that I...
_____
_____
_____

How do you feel today?:

- ☐ Happy
- ☐ Sad
- ☐ Stressed
- ☐ Energized
- ☐ Tired
- ☐ Stressed
- ☐ Fearful
- ☐ Angry

- ☐ Peaceful
- ☐ Disappointed
- ☐ Anxious
- ☐ Annoyed
- ☐ Hopeful
- ☐ Calm
- ☐ Productive
- ☐ Excited

- ☐ Negative
- ☐ Strong
- ☐ Inspired
- ☐ Thankful
- ☐ Loving
- ☐ Loved
- ☐ _____
- ☐ _____

_____
_____

What about today has been better than yesterday?
_____
_____
_____
_____
_____
_____
_____

DAILY
Gratitude

DATE : ____ ____ ____

∞∞∞∞∞∞∞∞∞∞∞∞∞∞∞∞∞∞∞∞∞∞∞∞∞∞∞∞∞∞∞∞∞∞∞∞

I am grateful for...

_____
_____
_____
_____

How many of your basic needs do you not have to worry about meeting today?

_____
_____
_____
_____
_____

How do you feel today?:

- ☐ Happy
- ☐ Sad
- ☐ Stressed
- ☐ Energized
- ☐ Tired
- ☐ Stressed
- ☐ Fearful
- ☐ Angry

- ☐ Peaceful
- ☐ Disappointed
- ☐ Anxious
- ☐ Annoyed
- ☐ Hopeful
- ☐ Calm
- ☐ Productive
- ☐ Excited

- ☐ Negative
- ☐ Strong
- ☐ Inspired
- ☐ Thankful
- ☐ Loving
- ☐ Loved
- ☐ _____
- ☐ _____

_____
_____

> **Take Action:** Use social media to describe one unexpected blessing you've received recently.

☐ Completed

DAILY
Gratitude

DATE : ____ ____ ____

I am grateful for...

_____
_____
_____
_____

Positive Affirmation: I am...

_____
_____
_____

How do you feel today?:

- ☐ Happy
- ☐ Sad
- ☐ Stressed
- ☐ Energized
- ☐ Tired
- ☐ Stressed
- ☐ Fearful
- ☐ Angry

- ☐ Peaceful
- ☐ Disappointed
- ☐ Anxious
- ☐ Annoyed
- ☐ Hopeful
- ☐ Calm
- ☐ Productive
- ☐ Excited

- ☐ Negative
- ☐ Strong
- ☐ Inspired
- ☐ Thankful
- ☐ Loving
- ☐ Loved
- ☐ _____
- ☐ _____

Write about a person in you're life you're thankful for and why?

_____
_____
_____
_____
_____
_____

DAILY
Gratitude

DATE : ____ ____ ____

I am grateful for...

_____
_____
_____
_____

What are 5 small ways you can share your gratitude today?

_____
_____
_____
_____
_____
_____

How do you feel today?:

- ☐ Happy
- ☐ Sad
- ☐ Stressed
- ☐ Energized
- ☐ Tired
- ☐ Stressed
- ☐ Fearful
- ☐ Angry

- ☐ Peaceful
- ☐ Disappointed
- ☐ Anxious
- ☐ Annoyed
- ☐ Hopeful
- ☐ Calm
- ☐ Productive
- ☐ Excited

- ☐ Negative
- ☐ Strong
- ☐ Inspired
- ☐ Thankful
- ☐ Loving
- ☐ Loved
- ☐ _____
- ☐ _____

What are skills and abilities you are thankful for?

_____
_____
_____
_____

DAILY
Gratitude

DATE : ____ ____ ____

I am grateful for...
_____
_____
_____
_____

Today I'm proud that I...
_____
_____
_____

How do you feel today?:

- ☐ Happy
- ☐ Sad
- ☐ Stressed
- ☐ Energized
- ☐ Tired
- ☐ Stressed
- ☐ Fearful
- ☐ Angry

- ☐ Peaceful
- ☐ Disappointed
- ☐ Anxious
- ☐ Annoyed
- ☐ Hopeful
- ☐ Calm
- ☐ Productive
- ☐ Excited

- ☐ Negative
- ☐ Strong
- ☐ Inspired
- ☐ Thankful
- ☐ Loving
- ☐ Loved
- ☐ _____
- ☐ _____

_____
_____

What is there about a challenge that you're experiencing right now that you can be thankful for?
_____
_____
_____
_____
_____
_____
_____

DAILY
Gratitude

DATE : ____ ____ ____

◇◇

I am grateful for...

_____
_____
_____
_____

How is where you are in life today different than a year ago?

_____
_____
_____
_____
_____
_____
_____
_____
_____
_____
_____

How do you feel today?:

- ☐ Happy
- ☐ Sad
- ☐ Stressed
- ☐ Energized
- ☐ Tired
- ☐ Stressed
- ☐ Fearful
- ☐ Angry

- ☐ Peaceful
- ☐ Disappointed
- ☐ Anxious
- ☐ Annoyed
- ☐ Hopeful
- ☐ Calm
- ☐ Productive
- ☐ Excited

- ☐ Negative
- ☐ Strong
- ☐ Inspired
- ☐ Thankful
- ☐ Loving
- ☐ Loved
- ☐ _____
- ☐ _____

DAILY
Gratitude

DATE : ____ ____ ____

◇◇

"The major value in life is not what you get. The major value in life is what you become." — Jim Rohn

I am grateful for...
_____
_____

Write about one person you're extremely grateful for and why?
_____
_____
_____

How do you feel today?:

- ☐ Happy
- ☐ Sad
- ☐ Stressed
- ☐ Energized
- ☐ Tired
- ☐ Stressed
- ☐ Fearful
- ☐ Angry

- ☐ Peaceful
- ☐ Disappointed
- ☐ Anxious
- ☐ Annoyed
- ☐ Hopeful
- ☐ Calm
- ☐ Productive
- ☐ Excited

- ☐ Negative
- ☐ Strong
- ☐ Inspired
- ☐ Thankful
- ☐ Loving
- ☐ Loved
- ☐ _____
- ☐ _____

_____
_____

What are you taking for granted about your day to day that you can be grateful for?
_____
_____
_____
_____
_____
_____

DAILY
Gratitude

DATE : ___ ___ ___

I am grateful for...

_____
_____
_____
_____

List 5 people in your life that are hard to get along with, write down at least 1 quality about each of them you're grateful for.

_____
_____
_____
_____
_____
_____
_____
_____
_____
_____
_____
_____
_____
_____

What materialistic items are you most grateful for?

_____
_____
_____
_____
_____
_____
_____

DAILY
Gratitude

DATE : _____ _____ _____

◇◇

I am grateful for...
_____
_____
_____
_____

Today I'm proud that I...
_____
_____
_____

How do you feel today?:

☐ Happy   ☐ Peaceful   ☐ Negative
☐ Sad   ☐ Disappointed   ☐ Strong
☐ Stressed   ☐ Anxious   ☐ Inspired
☐ Energized   ☐ Annoyed   ☐ Thankful
☐ Tired   ☐ Hopeful   ☐ Loving
☐ Stressed   ☐ Calm   ☐ Loved
☐ Fearful   ☐ Productive   ☐ _____
☐ Angry   ☐ Excited   ☐ _____

Who has done something for your life this week that has made your life easier and how can you thank them?
_____
_____
_____
_____
_____
_____

DAILY
Gratitude

DATE : ____ ____ ____

◇◇◇

I am grateful for...
_____
_____
_____
_____

What foods and meals are you most thankful for?

_____
_____
_____
_____
_____

How do you feel today?:

☐ Happy   ☐ Peaceful   ☐ Negative
☐ Sad   ☐ Disappointed   ☐ Strong
☐ Stressed   ☐ Anxious   ☐ Inspired
☐ Energized   ☐ Annoyed   ☐ Thankful
☐ Tired   ☐ Hopeful   ☐ Loving
☐ Stressed   ☐ Calm   ☐ Loved
☐ Fearful   ☐ Productive   ☐ _____
☐ Angry   ☐ Excited   ☐ _____

_____
_____

⟩ Take Action: Text a thank you note to someone who wasn't expecting it.

☐ Completed

DAILY
Gratitude

DATE : ____ ____ ____

I am grateful for...

___
___
___
___

Positive Affirmation: I am...

___
___
___

How do you feel today?:

- ☐ Happy
- ☐ Sad
- ☐ Stressed
- ☐ Energized
- ☐ Tired
- ☐ Stressed
- ☐ Fearful
- ☐ Angry

- ☐ Peaceful
- ☐ Disappointed
- ☐ Anxious
- ☐ Annoyed
- ☐ Hopeful
- ☐ Calm
- ☐ Productive
- ☐ Excited

- ☐ Negative
- ☐ Strong
- ☐ Inspired
- ☐ Thankful
- ☐ Loving
- ☐ Loved
- ☐ _____
- ☐ _____

___
___

What part of your morning routine are you most thankful for?

___
___
___
___
___

DAILY
Gratitude

DATE : ____ ____ ____

◇◇◇

I am grateful for...

_____
_____
_____
_____

What is something you are grateful for that you learned this week?

_____
_____
_____
_____
_____
_____

How do you feel today?:

- ☐ Happy
- ☐ Sad
- ☐ Stressed
- ☐ Energized
- ☐ Tired
- ☐ Stressed
- ☐ Fearful
- ☐ Angry

- ☐ Peaceful
- ☐ Disappointed
- ☐ Anxious
- ☐ Annoyed
- ☐ Hopeful
- ☐ Calm
- ☐ Productive
- ☐ Excited

- ☐ Negative
- ☐ Strong
- ☐ Inspired
- ☐ Thankful
- ☐ Loving
- ☐ Loved
- ☐ _____
- ☐ _____

When was the last time you laughed uncontrollably? Relive the memory.

_____
_____
_____
_____

DAILY *Gratitude*

DATE : ____ ____ ____

I am grateful for...

_____
_____
_____
_____

Today I'm proud that I...

_____
_____
_____

How do you feel today?:

- ☐ Happy
- ☐ Sad
- ☐ Stressed
- ☐ Energized
- ☐ Tired
- ☐ Stressed
- ☐ Fearful
- ☐ Angry

- ☐ Peaceful
- ☐ Disappointed
- ☐ Anxious
- ☐ Annoyed
- ☐ Hopeful
- ☐ Calm
- ☐ Productive
- ☐ Excited

- ☐ Negative
- ☐ Strong
- ☐ Inspired
- ☐ Thankful
- ☐ Loving
- ☐ Loved
- ☐ _____
- ☐ _____

_____
_____

Who is a teacher or mentor whose wise advice you still implement?

_____
_____
_____
_____
_____
_____
_____

DAILY
Gratitude

DATE : ____ ____ ____

⋈⋈⋈

I am grateful for...

_____
_____
_____
_____

What's a relationship in your life that gives you lots of feelings of stability?

_____
_____
_____
_____
_____
_____
_____
_____
_____
_____

How do you feel today?:

☐ Happy	☐ Peaceful	☐ Negative
☐ Sad	☐ Disappointed	☐ Strong
☐ Stressed	☐ Anxious	☐ Inspired
☐ Energized	☐ Annoyed	☐ Thankful
☐ Tired	☐ Hopeful	☐ Loving
☐ Stressed	☐ Calm	☐ Loved
☐ Fearful	☐ Productive	☐ _____
☐ Angry	☐ Excited	☐ _____

DAILY
Gratitude

DATE : ____ ____ ____

◇◇

"Gratitude turns what we have into enough." – Anonymous

I am grateful for...
_____
_____
_____

What did I read or listen to today that added value to my life?
_____
_____
_____
_____

How do you feel today?:

☐ Happy	☐ Peaceful	☐ Negative
☐ Sad	☐ Disappointed	☐ Strong
☐ Stressed	☐ Anxious	☐ Inspired
☐ Energized	☐ Annoyed	☐ Thankful
☐ Tired	☐ Hopeful	☐ Loving
☐ Stressed	☐ Calm	☐ Loved
☐ Fearful	☐ Productive	☐ _____
☐ Angry	☐ Excited	☐ _____

_____
_____

What compliment did I receive today?
_____
_____
_____
_____
_____
_____

DAILY
Gratitude

DATE : ____ ____ ____

I am grateful for...
_____
_____
_____
_____

What's the silver lining to something that went wrong today?
_____
_____
_____
_____
_____
_____
_____
_____
_____
_____
_____
_____
_____
_____
_____

What positive emotions did I experience today?
_____
_____
_____
_____
_____
_____
_____
_____

DAILY
Gratitude

DATE : ____ ____ ____

I am grateful for...

_____
_____
_____
_____

Today I'm proud that I...

_____
_____
_____

How do you feel today?:

- ☐ Happy
- ☐ Sad
- ☐ Stressed
- ☐ Energized
- ☐ Tired
- ☐ Stressed
- ☐ Fearful
- ☐ Angry

- ☐ Peaceful
- ☐ Disappointed
- ☐ Anxious
- ☐ Annoyed
- ☐ Hopeful
- ☐ Calm
- ☐ Productive
- ☐ Excited

- ☐ Negative
- ☐ Strong
- ☐ Inspired
- ☐ Thankful
- ☐ Loving
- ☐ Loved
- ☐ _____
- ☐ _____

_____
_____

Have you had a chance to help someone recently, and how did that make you feel?

_____
_____
_____
_____
_____
_____
_____

DAILY
Gratitude

DATE : ____ ____ ____

◇◇

I am grateful for...

_____
_____
_____
_____

What are you taking for granted about your day to day that you could be thankful for?

_____
_____
_____
_____
_____
_____

How do you feel today?:

- ☐ Happy
- ☐ Sad
- ☐ Stressed
- ☐ Energized
- ☐ Tired
- ☐ Stressed
- ☐ Fearful
- ☐ Angry

- ☐ Peaceful
- ☐ Disappointed
- ☐ Anxious
- ☐ Annoyed
- ☐ Hopeful
- ☐ Calm
- ☐ Productive
- ☐ Excited

- ☐ Negative
- ☐ Strong
- ☐ Inspired
- ☐ Thankful
- ☐ Loving
- ☐ Loved
- ☐ _____
- ☐ _____

_____
_____

> Take Action: Buy someone lunch this week.

☐ Task Completed

DAILY
Gratitude

DATE : ____ ____ ___

◇◇◇

I am grateful for...
_____
_____
_____
_____

Positive Affirmation: I am...
_____
_____
_____

How do you feel today?:

- ☐ Happy
- ☐ Sad
- ☐ Stressed
- ☐ Energized
- ☐ Tired
- ☐ Stressed
- ☐ Fearful
- ☐ Angry

- ☐ Peaceful
- ☐ Disappointed
- ☐ Anxious
- ☐ Annoyed
- ☐ Hopeful
- ☐ Calm
- ☐ Productive
- ☐ Excited

- ☐ Negative
- ☐ Strong
- ☐ Inspired
- ☐ Thankful
- ☐ Loving
- ☐ Loved
- ☐ _____
- ☐ _____

_____
_____

What's an aspect of how you were parented for which you feel grateful?
_____
_____
_____
_____
_____
_____
_____

DAILY
Gratitude

DATE : ____ ____ ____

∞∞

I am grateful for...
_____
_____
_____
_____

What's something that you just accomplished? How do you feel about it can be big or small.
_____
_____
_____
_____
_____
_____

How do you feel today?:

- ☐ Happy
- ☐ Sad
- ☐ Stressed
- ☐ Energized
- ☐ Tired
- ☐ Stressed
- ☐ Fearful
- ☐ Angry

- ☐ Peaceful
- ☐ Disappointed
- ☐ Anxious
- ☐ Annoyed
- ☐ Hopeful
- ☐ Calm
- ☐ Productive
- ☐ Excited

- ☐ Negative
- ☐ Strong
- ☐ Inspired
- ☐ Thankful
- ☐ Loving
- ☐ Loved
- ☐ _____
- ☐ _____

I could have made today better by:
_____
_____
_____
_____

DAILY
Gratitude

DATE : ____ ____ ____

◇◇

I am grateful for...
_____
_____
_____
_____

Today I'm proud that I...
_____
_____
_____

How do you feel today?:

☐ Happy   ☐ Peaceful   ☐ Negative
☐ Sad   ☐ Disappointed   ☐ Strong
☐ Stressed   ☐ Anxious   ☐ Inspired
☐ Energized   ☐ Annoyed   ☐ Thankful
☐ Tired   ☐ Hopeful   ☐ Loving
☐ Stressed   ☐ Calm   ☐ Loved
☐ Fearful   ☐ Productive   ☐ _____
☐ Angry   ☐ Excited   ☐ _____

_____

What's a stressor you're grateful to have put behind you this year?
_____
_____
_____
_____
_____
_____
_____

DAILY
Gratitude

DATE : ____ ____ ____

∞∞

I am grateful for...

_____
_____
_____
_____

On days when I'm feeling blue, what is something I can do?

_____
_____
_____
_____
_____
_____

How do you feel today?:

- ☐ Happy
- ☐ Sad
- ☐ Stressed
- ☐ Energized
- ☐ Tired
- ☐ Stressed
- ☐ Fearful
- ☐ Angry

- ☐ Peaceful
- ☐ Disappointed
- ☐ Anxious
- ☐ Annoyed
- ☐ Hopeful
- ☐ Calm
- ☐ Productive
- ☐ Excited

- ☐ Negative
- ☐ Strong
- ☐ Inspired
- ☐ Thankful
- ☐ Loving
- ☐ Loved
- ☐ _____
- ☐ _____

Notes:

_____
_____
_____
_____

DAILY *Gratitude*

DATE : ____ ____ ____

◊◊

"Open your eyes, look within. Are you satisfied with the life you're living?"
— Bob Marley

I am grateful for...

_____
_____
_____

Am I holding on to something I need to let go of?

_____
_____
_____
_____

How do you feel today?:

☐ Happy   ☐ Peaceful   ☐ Negative
☐ Sad   ☐ Disappointed   ☐ Strong
☐ Stressed   ☐ Anxious   ☐ Inspired
☐ Energized   ☐ Annoyed   ☐ Thankful
☐ Tired   ☐ Hopeful   ☐ Loving
☐ Stressed   ☐ Calm   ☐ Loved
☐ Fearful   ☐ Productive   ☐ _____
☐ Angry   ☐ Excited   ☐ _____

_____
_____

How have you used your talents recently, and what have you enjoyed about doing that?

_____
_____
_____
_____
_____
_____

DAILY
Gratitude

DATE : ____ ____ ____

◇◇◇

I am grateful for...

_____
_____
_____
_____

What's something you've enjoyed about doing your job recently?

_____
_____
_____
_____
_____
_____
_____
_____
_____
_____
_____
_____
_____
_____

What's something you witnessed recently that reminded you that life is good?

_____
_____
_____
_____
_____
_____
_____

DAILY
Gratitude

DATE : ____ ____ ____

∞∞∞∞∞∞∞∞∞∞∞∞∞∞∞∞∞∞∞∞∞∞∞∞∞∞∞∞∞∞∞

I am grateful for...

_____
_____
_____
_____

Today I'm proud that I...

_____
_____
_____

How do you feel today?:

- ☐ Happy
- ☐ Sad
- ☐ Stressed
- ☐ Energized
- ☐ Tired
- ☐ Stressed
- ☐ Fearful
- ☐ Angry

- ☐ Peaceful
- ☐ Disappointed
- ☐ Anxious
- ☐ Annoyed
- ☐ Hopeful
- ☐ Calm
- ☐ Productive
- ☐ Excited

- ☐ Negative
- ☐ Strong
- ☐ Inspired
- ☐ Thankful
- ☐ Loving
- ☐ Loved
- ☐ _____
- ☐ _____

_____
_____

What's the best thing about your home, and have you taken time to enjoy it recently?

_____
_____
_____
_____
_____
_____
_____

DAILY
Gratitude

DATE : ____ ____ ____

◇◇◇

I am grateful for...

_____
_____
_____
_____

What movie, book, blog, or article affected your life for the better recently?

_____
_____
_____
_____
_____
_____

How do you feel today?:

- ☐ Happy
- ☐ Sad
- ☐ Stressed
- ☐ Energized
- ☐ Tired
- ☐ Stressed
- ☐ Fearful
- ☐ Angry

- ☐ Peaceful
- ☐ Disappointed
- ☐ Anxious
- ☐ Annoyed
- ☐ Hopeful
- ☐ Calm
- ☐ Productive
- ☐ Excited

- ☐ Negative
- ☐ Strong
- ☐ Inspired
- ☐ Thankful
- ☐ Loving
- ☐ Loved
- ☐ _____
- ☐ _____

_____
_____

⊙ Take Action: Text someone that you were thinking about today.

☐ Seriously, Send the text.

DAILY
Gratitude

DATE : ____ ____ ____

◇◇

I am grateful for...

_____
_____
_____
_____

Positive Affirmation: I am...

_____
_____
_____

How do you feel today?:

☐ Happy	☐ Peaceful	☐ Negative
☐ Sad	☐ Disappointed	☐ Strong
☐ Stressed	☐ Anxious	☐ Inspired
☐ Energized	☐ Annoyed	☐ Thankful
☐ Tired	☐ Hopeful	☐ Loving
☐ Stressed	☐ Calm	☐ Loved
☐ Fearful	☐ Productive	☐ _____
☐ Angry	☐ Excited	☐ _____

What's something you have easy access to that always improves your mood,

_____
_____
_____
_____
_____
_____
_____

DAILY
Gratitude

DATE : ____ ____ ____

∞∞∞

I am grateful for...

_____
_____
_____
_____

Have you recently imagined a worst-case scenario that didn't actually happen?

_____
_____
_____
_____
_____
_____

How do you feel today?:

☐ Happy	☐ Peaceful	☐ Negative
☐ Sad	☐ Disappointed	☐ Strong
☐ Stressed	☐ Anxious	☐ Inspired
☐ Energized	☐ Annoyed	☐ Thankful
☐ Tired	☐ Hopeful	☐ Loving
☐ Stressed	☐ Calm	☐ Loved
☐ Fearful	☐ Productive	☐ _____
☐ Angry	☐ Excited	☐ _____

I could have made today better by:

_____
_____
_____
_____

DAILY *Gratitude*

DATE : ____ ____ ____

◇◇

I am grateful for...

_____
_____
_____
_____

Today I'm proud that I...

_____
_____
_____

How do you feel today?:

☐ Happy	☐ Peaceful	☐ Negative
☐ Sad	☐ Disappointed	☐ Strong
☐ Stressed	☐ Anxious	☐ Inspired
☐ Energized	☐ Annoyed	☐ Thankful
☐ Tired	☐ Hopeful	☐ Loving
☐ Stressed	☐ Calm	☐ Loved
☐ Fearful	☐ Productive	☐ _____
☐ Angry	☐ Excited	☐ _____

_____

What choices have you made in the last five years that you'd thank yourself for making?

_____
_____
_____
_____
_____
_____
_____

DAILY
Gratitude

DATE : _____ _____ _____

I am grateful for...

_____
_____
_____
_____

What negative was I able to turn into a positive today?

_____
_____
_____
_____
_____
_____
_____
_____
_____
_____

How do you feel today?:

- ☐ Happy
- ☐ Sad
- ☐ Stressed
- ☐ Energized
- ☐ Tired
- ☐ Stressed
- ☐ Fearful
- ☐ Angry

- ☐ Peaceful
- ☐ Disappointed
- ☐ Anxious
- ☐ Annoyed
- ☐ Hopeful
- ☐ Calm
- ☐ Productive
- ☐ Excited

- ☐ Negative
- ☐ Strong
- ☐ Inspired
- ☐ Thankful
- ☐ Loving
- ☐ Loved
- ☐ _____
- ☐ _____

DAILY
Gratitude

DATE : ____ ____ ____

◇◇

"Our life is what our thoughts make it." — Marcus Aurelius

I am grateful for...

_____
_____
_____

What weakness was I able to keep in check today?

_____
_____
_____
_____

How do you feel today?:

- ☐ Happy
- ☐ Sad
- ☐ Stressed
- ☐ Energized
- ☐ Tired
- ☐ Stressed
- ☐ Fearful
- ☐ Angry

- ☐ Peaceful
- ☐ Disappointed
- ☐ Anxious
- ☐ Annoyed
- ☐ Hopeful
- ☐ Calm
- ☐ Productive
- ☐ Excited

- ☐ Negative
- ☐ Strong
- ☐ Inspired
- ☐ Thankful
- ☐ Loving
- ☐ Loved
- ☐ _____
- ☐ _____

_____
_____

How did I feel appreciated today?

_____
_____
_____
_____
_____
_____

DAILY
Gratitude

DATE : ____ ____ ____

◇◇

I am grateful for...
_____
_____
_____
_____

What's something you're looking forward to in the future?
_____
_____
_____
_____
_____
_____
_____
_____
_____
_____
_____
_____
_____
_____

How did I show myself compassion today?
_____
_____
_____
_____
_____
_____
_____

DAILY
Gratitude

DATE : ____ ____ ____

◇◇

I am grateful for...

_____
_____
_____
_____

Today I'm proud that I...

_____
_____
_____

How do you feel today?:

- ☐ Happy
- ☐ Sad
- ☐ Stressed
- ☐ Energized
- ☐ Tired
- ☐ Stressed
- ☐ Fearful
- ☐ Angry

- ☐ Peaceful
- ☐ Disappointed
- ☐ Anxious
- ☐ Annoyed
- ☐ Hopeful
- ☐ Calm
- ☐ Productive
- ☐ Excited

- ☐ Negative
- ☐ Strong
- ☐ Inspired
- ☐ Thankful
- ☐ Loving
- ☐ Loved
- ☐ _____
- ☐ _____

_____
_____

What's the season you're most thankful for, and what's your favorite part of each season?

_____
_____
_____
_____
_____
_____
_____

DAILY *Gratitude*

DATE : ____ ____ ____

I am grateful for...
_____
_____
_____
_____

Name three days in your life that you feel especially grateful for.
_____
_____
_____
_____
_____
_____

How do you feel today?:

- ☐ Happy
- ☐ Sad
- ☐ Stressed
- ☐ Energized
- ☐ Tired
- ☐ Stressed
- ☐ Fearful
- ☐ Angry

- ☐ Peaceful
- ☐ Disappointed
- ☐ Anxious
- ☐ Annoyed
- ☐ Hopeful
- ☐ Calm
- ☐ Productive
- ☐ Excited

- ☐ Negative
- ☐ Strong
- ☐ Inspired
- ☐ Thankful
- ☐ Loving
- ☐ Loved
- ☐ _____
- ☐ _____

_____
_____

> Take Action: Compliment yourself—say it while looking in the mirror, write it in a journal, or jot it on a sticky note and put it on your refrigerator.

☐ Completed

DAILY
Gratitude

DATE : ____ ____ ____

◇◇

I am grateful for...

_____
_____
_____
_____

Positive Affirmation: I am...

_____
_____
_____

How do you feel today?:

- ☐ Happy
- ☐ Sad
- ☐ Stressed
- ☐ Energized
- ☐ Tired
- ☐ Stressed
- ☐ Fearful
- ☐ Angry

- ☐ Peaceful
- ☐ Disappointed
- ☐ Anxious
- ☐ Annoyed
- ☐ Hopeful
- ☐ Calm
- ☐ Productive
- ☐ Excited

- ☐ Negative
- ☐ Strong
- ☐ Inspired
- ☐ Thankful
- ☐ Loving
- ☐ Loved
- ☐ _____
- ☐ _____

_____

What event or interaction made you feel good about yourself recently?

_____
_____
_____
_____
_____
_____

DAILY *Gratitude*

DATE : ____ ____ ____

∞∞

I am grateful for...

_____
_____
_____
_____

What are your 3 new things you want to learn?

_____
_____
_____
_____
_____
_____

How do you feel today?:

- ☐ Happy
- ☐ Sad
- ☐ Stressed
- ☐ Energized
- ☐ Tired
- ☐ Stressed
- ☐ Fearful
- ☐ Angry

- ☐ Peaceful
- ☐ Disappointed
- ☐ Anxious
- ☐ Annoyed
- ☐ Hopeful
- ☐ Calm
- ☐ Productive
- ☐ Excited

- ☐ Negative
- ☐ Strong
- ☐ Inspired
- ☐ Thankful
- ☐ Loving
- ☐ Loved
- ☐ _____
- ☐ _____

I could have made today better by:

_____
_____
_____
_____

DAILY
Gratitude

DATE : ____ ____ ____

◇◇◇

I am grateful for...

_____
_____
_____
_____

Today I'm proud that I...

_____
_____
_____

How do you feel today?:

☐ Happy	☐ Peaceful	☐ Negative
☐ Sad	☐ Disappointed	☐ Strong
☐ Stressed	☐ Anxious	☐ Inspired
☐ Energized	☐ Annoyed	☐ Thankful
☐ Tired	☐ Hopeful	☐ Loving
☐ Stressed	☐ Calm	☐ Loved
☐ Fearful	☐ Productive	☐ _____
☐ Angry	☐ Excited	☐ _____

_____

What are three things your arms or legs allow you to do th you enjoy?

_____
_____
_____
_____
_____
_____

DAILY
Gratitude

DATE : ____ ____ ____

∞∞

I am grateful for...

_____
_____
_____
_____

What am I taking for granted that, if I stop to think about it, I am grateful for?

_____
_____
_____
_____
_____
_____
_____
_____
_____
_____

How do you feel today?:

☐ Happy	☐ Peaceful	☐ Negative
☐ Sad	☐ Disappointed	☐ Strong
☐ Stressed	☐ Anxious	☐ Inspired
☐ Energized	☐ Annoyed	☐ Thankful
☐ Tired	☐ Hopeful	☐ Loving
☐ Stressed	☐ Calm	☐ Loved
☐ Fearful	☐ Productive	☐ _____
☐ Angry	☐ Excited	☐ _____

DAILY
Gratitude

DATE : ____ ____ ____

◇◇

"The more you praise and celebrate your life, the more there is in life to celebrate."
— Oprah Winfrey

I am grateful for...
_____
_____
_____

What's one thoughtful thing someone did for you recently?
_____
_____
_____
_____

How do you feel today?:

☐ Happy	☐ Peaceful	☐ Negative
☐ Sad	☐ Disappointed	☐ Strong
☐ Stressed	☐ Anxious	☐ Inspired
☐ Energized	☐ Annoyed	☐ Thankful
☐ Tired	☐ Hopeful	☐ Loving
☐ Stressed	☐ Calm	☐ Loved
☐ Fearful	☐ Productive	☐ _____
☐ Angry	☐ Excited	☐ _____

_____
_____

What abilities do I have that I'm grateful for?
_____
_____
_____
_____
_____
_____
_____

DAILY
Gratitude

DATE : ____ ____ ____

∞∞

I am grateful for...

_____
_____
_____
_____

What insights have I gained that I am grateful for?

_____
_____
_____
_____
_____
_____
_____
_____
_____
_____
_____
_____
_____
_____
_____

Where can I help people more?

_____
_____
_____
_____
_____
_____
_____
_____

DAILY
Gratitude

DATE : ____ ____ ____

∞∞∞∞∞∞∞∞∞∞∞∞∞∞∞∞∞∞∞∞∞∞∞∞∞∞∞∞∞∞∞∞∞∞∞∞

I am grateful for...
_____
_____
_____
_____

Today I'm proud that I...
_____
_____
_____

How do you feel today?:

- ☐ Happy
- ☐ Sad
- ☐ Stressed
- ☐ Energized
- ☐ Tired
- ☐ Stressed
- ☐ Fearful
- ☐ Angry

- ☐ Peaceful
- ☐ Disappointed
- ☐ Anxious
- ☐ Annoyed
- ☐ Hopeful
- ☐ Calm
- ☐ Productive
- ☐ Excited

- ☐ Negative
- ☐ Strong
- ☐ Inspired
- ☐ Thankful
- ☐ Loving
- ☐ Loved
- ☐ _____
- ☐ _____

_____
_____

Who has done something for your life this week that has made your life easier and how can you thank them?
_____
_____
_____
_____
_____
_____
_____

DAILY
Gratitude

DATE : ____ ____ ____

∞∞

I am grateful for...

_____
_____
_____
_____

What's something that most people find weird, but you actually love.

_____
_____
_____
_____
_____
_____

How do you feel today?:

- ☐ Happy
- ☐ Sad
- ☐ Stressed
- ☐ Energized
- ☐ Tired
- ☐ Stressed
- ☐ Fearful
- ☐ Angry

- ☐ Peaceful
- ☐ Disappointed
- ☐ Anxious
- ☐ Annoyed
- ☐ Hopeful
- ☐ Calm
- ☐ Productive
- ☐ Excited

- ☐ Negative
- ☐ Strong
- ☐ Inspired
- ☐ Thankful
- ☐ Loving
- ☐ Loved
- ☐ _____
- ☐ _____

_____
_____

> Take Action: Commit to a complaint free day.

☐ Completed

DAILY
Gratitude

DATE : ____ ____ ____

◇◇

I am grateful for...

_____
_____
_____
_____

Positive Affirmation: I am...

_____
_____
_____

How do you feel today?:

- ☐ Happy
- ☐ Sad
- ☐ Stressed
- ☐ Energized
- ☐ Tired
- ☐ Stressed
- ☐ Fearful
- ☐ Angry

- ☐ Peaceful
- ☐ Disappointed
- ☐ Anxious
- ☐ Annoyed
- ☐ Hopeful
- ☐ Calm
- ☐ Productive
- ☐ Excited

- ☐ Negative
- ☐ Strong
- ☐ Inspired
- ☐ Thankful
- ☐ Loving
- ☐ Loved
- ☐ _____
- ☐ _____

_____
_____

What, from this year, do you feel most grateful for?

_____
_____
_____
_____
_____

DAILY
Gratitude

DATE : ____ ____ ____

◇◇

I am grateful for...
_____
_____
_____

What's something that you bought recently that you're grateful for?
_____
_____
_____
_____
_____

How do you feel today?:

☐ Happy   ☐ Peaceful   ☐ Negative
☐ Sad   ☐ Disappointed   ☐ Strong
☐ Stressed   ☐ Anxious   ☐ Inspired
☐ Energized   ☐ Annoyed   ☐ Thankful
☐ Tired   ☐ Hopeful   ☐ Loving
☐ Stressed   ☐ Calm   ☐ Loved
☐ Fearful   ☐ Productive   ☐ _____
☐ Angry   ☐ Excited   ☐ _____

What's something or someone that makes you feel safe?
_____
_____
_____
_____

DAILY
Gratitude

DATE : ____ ____ ____

◊◊

I am grateful for...

_____
_____
_____
_____

Today I'm proud that I...

_____
_____
_____

How do you feel today?:

- ☐ Happy
- ☐ Sad
- ☐ Stressed
- ☐ Energized
- ☐ Tired
- ☐ Stressed
- ☐ Fearful
- ☐ Angry

- ☐ Peaceful
- ☐ Disappointed
- ☐ Anxious
- ☐ Annoyed
- ☐ Hopeful
- ☐ Calm
- ☐ Productive
- ☐ Excited

- ☐ Negative
- ☐ Strong
- ☐ Inspired
- ☐ Thankful
- ☐ Loving
- ☐ Loved
- ☐ _____
- ☐ _____

_____

What's a simple pleasure that you're grateful for?

_____
_____
_____
_____
_____
_____

DAILY
Gratitude

DATE : ____ ____ ____

I am grateful for...

_____
_____
_____
_____

What opportunities have changed your life?

_____
_____
_____
_____
_____
_____
_____
_____
_____
_____
_____

How do you feel today?:

☐ Happy	☐ Peaceful	☐ Negative
☐ Sad	☐ Disappointed	☐ Strong
☐ Stressed	☐ Anxious	☐ Inspired
☐ Energized	☐ Annoyed	☐ Thankful
☐ Tired	☐ Hopeful	☐ Loving
☐ Stressed	☐ Calm	☐ Loved
☐ Fearful	☐ Productive	☐ _____
☐ Angry	☐ Excited	☐ _____

DAILY
Gratitude

DATE : ____ ____ ____

"The way of success is the way of continuous pursuit of knowledge." – Napoleon Hill

I am grateful for...
_____
_____

How do you like to spend your spare time?
_____
_____
_____

How do you feel today?:

☐ Happy	☐ Peaceful	☐ Negative
☐ Sad	☐ Disappointed	☐ Strong
☐ Stressed	☐ Anxious	☐ Inspired
☐ Energized	☐ Annoyed	☐ Thankful
☐ Tired	☐ Hopeful	☐ Loving
☐ Stressed	☐ Calm	☐ Loved
☐ Fearful	☐ Productive	☐ _____
☐ Angry	☐ Excited	☐ _____

_____
_____

What compliment did I receive today?
_____
_____
_____
_____
_____

DAILY
Gratitude

DATE : ____ ____ ____

∞∞∞

I am grateful for...

What inspires you to keep going when it's hard?

When did you last feel really at peace?

DAILY
Gratitude

DATE : ____ ____ ____

I am grateful for...
_____
_____
_____
_____

Today I'm proud that I...
_____
_____
_____

How do you feel today?:

- ☐ Happy
- ☐ Sad
- ☐ Stressed
- ☐ Energized
- ☐ Tired
- ☐ Stressed
- ☐ Fearful
- ☐ Angry

- ☐ Peaceful
- ☐ Disappointed
- ☐ Anxious
- ☐ Annoyed
- ☐ Hopeful
- ☐ Calm
- ☐ Productive
- ☐ Excited

- ☐ Negative
- ☐ Strong
- ☐ Inspired
- ☐ Thankful
- ☐ Loving
- ☐ Loved
- ☐ _____
- ☐ _____

_____
_____

Who is the most positive, inspiring person you know?
_____
_____
_____
_____
_____
_____

DAILY *Gratitude*

DATE : ____ ____ ____

◇◇

I am grateful for...
_____
_____
_____
_____

What traditions did you enjoy as a child?
_____
_____
_____
_____
_____

How do you feel today?:

☐ Happy	☐ Peaceful	☐ Negative
☐ Sad	☐ Disappointed	☐ Strong
☐ Stressed	☐ Anxious	☐ Inspired
☐ Energized	☐ Annoyed	☐ Thankful
☐ Tired	☐ Hopeful	☐ Loving
☐ Stressed	☐ Calm	☐ Loved
☐ Fearful	☐ Productive	☐ _____
☐ Angry	☐ Excited	☐ _____

_____
_____

⊳ Say thank you for the little things your loved ones do for you, things you normally take for granted.

☐ Task Completed

DAILY
Gratitude

DATE : _____ _____ _____

I am grateful for...

_____
_____
_____
_____

Positive Affirmation: I am...

_____
_____
_____

How do you feel today?:

- ☐ Happy
- ☐ Sad
- ☐ Stressed
- ☐ Energized
- ☐ Tired
- ☐ Stressed
- ☐ Fearful
- ☐ Angry

- ☐ Peaceful
- ☐ Disappointed
- ☐ Anxious
- ☐ Annoyed
- ☐ Hopeful
- ☐ Calm
- ☐ Productive
- ☐ Excited

- ☐ Negative
- ☐ Strong
- ☐ Inspired
- ☐ Thankful
- ☐ Loving
- ☐ Loved
- ☐ _____
- ☐ _____

What do you enjoy about your career?

_____
_____
_____
_____
_____
_____
_____

DAILY
Gratitude

DATE : ____ ____ ____

◇◇

I am grateful for...

_____
_____
_____
_____

When did you last feel pure excitement?

_____
_____
_____
_____
_____

How do you feel today?:

☐ Happy	☐ Peaceful	☐ Negative
☐ Sad	☐ Disappointed	☐ Strong
☐ Stressed	☐ Anxious	☐ Inspired
☐ Energized	☐ Annoyed	☐ Thankful
☐ Tired	☐ Hopeful	☐ Loving
☐ Stressed	☐ Calm	☐ Loved
☐ Fearful	☐ Productive	☐ _____
☐ Angry	☐ Excited	☐ _____

I could have made today better by:

_____
_____
_____
_____

DAILY
Gratitude

DATE : ____ ____ ____

∞∞∞∞∞∞∞∞∞∞∞∞∞∞∞∞∞∞∞∞∞∞∞∞∞∞∞∞∞∞∞∞∞∞∞∞∞∞

I am grateful for...
_____
_____
_____
_____

Today I'm proud that I...
_____
_____
_____

How do you feel today?:

- ☐ Happy
- ☐ Sad
- ☐ Stressed
- ☐ Energized
- ☐ Tired
- ☐ Stressed
- ☐ Fearful
- ☐ Angry

- ☐ Peaceful
- ☐ Disappointed
- ☐ Anxious
- ☐ Annoyed
- ☐ Hopeful
- ☐ Calm
- ☐ Productive
- ☐ Excited

- ☐ Negative
- ☐ Strong
- ☐ Inspired
- ☐ Thankful
- ☐ Loving
- ☐ Loved
- ☐ _____
- ☐ _____

_____
_____

What character trait do you love most about yourself?
_____
_____
_____
_____
_____
_____
_____

DAILY
Gratitude

DATE : ____ ____ ____

◇◇◇

I am grateful for...

_____
_____
_____
_____

On days when I'm feeling blue, what is something I can do?

_____
_____
_____
_____
_____
_____

How do you feel today?:

- ☐ Happy
- ☐ Sad
- ☐ Stressed
- ☐ Energized
- ☐ Tired
- ☐ Stressed
- ☐ Fearful
- ☐ Angry
- ☐ Peaceful
- ☐ Disappointed
- ☐ Anxious
- ☐ Annoyed
- ☐ Hopeful
- ☐ Calm
- ☐ Productive
- ☐ Excited
- ☐ Negative
- ☐ Strong
- ☐ Inspired
- ☐ Thankful
- ☐ Loving
- ☐ Loved
- ☐ _____
- ☐ _____

Notes:

_____
_____
_____
_____

DAILY
Gratitude

DATE : ____ ____ ____

"You've been armed with strength for every battle. The forces that are for you are greater than forces against you." — Joel Osteen

I am grateful for...
___
___
___

What's physical attribute do you love most about yourself?
___
___
___
___

How do you feel today?:

- ☐ Happy
- ☐ Sad
- ☐ Stressed
- ☐ Energized
- ☐ Tired
- ☐ Stressed
- ☐ Fearful
- ☐ Angry

- ☐ Peaceful
- ☐ Disappointed
- ☐ Anxious
- ☐ Annoyed
- ☐ Hopeful
- ☐ Calm
- ☐ Productive
- ☐ Excited

- ☐ Negative
- ☐ Strong
- ☐ Inspired
- ☐ Thankful
- ☐ Loving
- ☐ Loved
- ☐ _____
- ☐ _____

___
___

What is a fear you're grateful to have overcome?
___
___
___
___
___

DAILY
Gratitude

DATE : ____ ____ ____

◇◇

I am grateful for...
_____
_____
_____
_____

What is a risk that you're grateful you took?
_____
_____
_____
_____
_____
_____
_____
_____
_____
_____
_____
_____
_____
_____

What is something you have now, which you didn't have a year ago?
_____
_____
_____
_____
_____
_____
_____

DAILY
Gratitude

DATE : ____ ____ ____

I am grateful for...

_____
_____
_____
_____

Today I'm proud that I...

_____
_____
_____

How do you feel today?:

☐ Happy	☐ Peaceful	☐ Negative
☐ Sad	☐ Disappointed	☐ Strong
☐ Stressed	☐ Anxious	☐ Inspired
☐ Energized	☐ Annoyed	☐ Thankful
☐ Tired	☐ Hopeful	☐ Loving
☐ Stressed	☐ Calm	☐ Loved
☐ Fearful	☐ Productive	☐ _____
☐ Angry	☐ Excited	☐ _____

_____
_____

What's the last thing you were gifted? Who gifted it to you? How did it make you feel?

_____
_____
_____
_____
_____
_____
_____

DAILY
Gratitude

DATE : ____ ____ ____

I am grateful for...

_____
_____
_____
_____

What is a luxury you are thankful for?

_____
_____
_____
_____
_____

How do you feel today?:

☐ Happy	☐ Peaceful	☐ Negative
☐ Sad	☐ Disappointed	☐ Strong
☐ Stressed	☐ Anxious	☐ Inspired
☐ Energized	☐ Annoyed	☐ Thankful
☐ Tired	☐ Hopeful	☐ Loving
☐ Stressed	☐ Calm	☐ Loved
☐ Fearful	☐ Productive	☐ _____
☐ Angry	☐ Excited	☐ _____

_____
_____

⊙ Take Action: Call your grandparents today if they are still alive, if not call an old friend.

☐ Completed

DAILY
Gratitude

DATE : _____ / _____ / _____

◇◇

I am grateful for...
_____
_____
_____
_____

Positive Affirmation: I am...
_____
_____
_____

How do you feel today?:

- ☐ Happy
- ☐ Sad
- ☐ Stressed
- ☐ Energized
- ☐ Tired
- ☐ Stressed
- ☐ Fearful
- ☐ Angry

- ☐ Peaceful
- ☐ Disappointed
- ☐ Anxious
- ☐ Annoyed
- ☐ Hopeful
- ☐ Calm
- ☐ Productive
- ☐ Excited

- ☐ Negative
- ☐ Strong
- ☐ Inspired
- ☐ Thankful
- ☐ Loving
- ☐ Loved
- ☐ _____
- ☐ _____

_____
_____

What positive change has happened in the past year?
_____
_____
_____
_____
_____
_____
_____
_____

DAILY
Gratitude

DATE : ____ ____ ____

◇◇◇

I am grateful for...

_____
_____
_____
_____

What goal are you thankful to be able to focus on at this time?

_____
_____
_____
_____
_____
_____

How do you feel today?:

- ☐ Happy
- ☐ Sad
- ☐ Stressed
- ☐ Energized
- ☐ Tired
- ☐ Stressed
- ☐ Fearful
- ☐ Angry

- ☐ Peaceful
- ☐ Disappointed
- ☐ Anxious
- ☐ Annoyed
- ☐ Hopeful
- ☐ Calm
- ☐ Productive
- ☐ Excited

- ☐ Negative
- ☐ Strong
- ☐ Inspired
- ☐ Thankful
- ☐ Loving
- ☐ Loved
- ☐ _____
- ☐ _____

I could have made today better by:

_____
_____
_____
_____

DAILY
Gratitude

DATE : ____ ____ ____

I am grateful for...

_____
_____
_____
_____

Today I'm proud that I...

_____
_____
_____

How do you feel today?:

- ☐ Happy
- ☐ Sad
- ☐ Stressed
- ☐ Energized
- ☐ Tired
- ☐ Stressed
- ☐ Fearful
- ☐ Angry

- ☐ Peaceful
- ☐ Disappointed
- ☐ Anxious
- ☐ Annoyed
- ☐ Hopeful
- ☐ Calm
- ☐ Productive
- ☐ Excited

- ☐ Negative
- ☐ Strong
- ☐ Inspired
- ☐ Thankful
- ☐ Loving
- ☐ Loved
- ☐ _____
- ☐ _____

_____
_____

What did I read or listen to today that added value to my life?

_____
_____
_____
_____
_____
_____
_____

DAILY
Gratitude

DATE : ____ ____ ____

◇◇

I am grateful for...
_____
_____
_____
_____

How did I move an important goal forward today?
_____
_____
_____
_____
_____
_____
_____
_____
_____
_____

How do you feel today?:

- ☐ Happy
- ☐ Sad
- ☐ Stressed
- ☐ Energized
- ☐ Tired
- ☐ Stressed
- ☐ Fearful
- ☐ Angry

- ☐ Peaceful
- ☐ Disappointed
- ☐ Anxious
- ☐ Annoyed
- ☐ Hopeful
- ☐ Calm
- ☐ Productive
- ☐ Excited

- ☐ Negative
- ☐ Strong
- ☐ Inspired
- ☐ Thankful
- ☐ Loving
- ☐ Loved
- ☐ _____
- ☐ _____

DAILY
Gratitude

DATE : ____ ____ ____

"Do what you are scared to do and watch your confidence grow."
— Grant Cardone

I am grateful for...
_____
_____
_____

How did I feel appreciated today?
_____
_____
_____
_____

How do you feel today?:

- ☐ Happy
- ☐ Sad
- ☐ Stressed
- ☐ Energized
- ☐ Tired
- ☐ Stressed
- ☐ Fearful
- ☐ Angry

- ☐ Peaceful
- ☐ Disappointed
- ☐ Anxious
- ☐ Annoyed
- ☐ Hopeful
- ☐ Calm
- ☐ Productive
- ☐ Excited

- ☐ Negative
- ☐ Strong
- ☐ Inspired
- ☐ Thankful
- ☐ Loving
- ☐ Loved
- ☐ _____
- ☐ _____

_____
_____

What positive habits did I engage in today?
_____
_____
_____
_____
_____
_____

DAILY
Gratitude

DATE : ____ ____ ____

I am grateful for...
_____
_____
_____
_____

What do you have in your life right now that others (that you know or around the world) do not?
_____
_____
_____
_____
_____
_____
_____
_____
_____
_____
_____
_____
_____
_____

How was I able to help others today?
_____
_____
_____
_____
_____
_____
_____

DAILY
Gratitude

DATE : ____ ____ ____

∞∞∞∞∞∞∞∞∞∞∞∞∞∞∞∞∞∞∞∞∞∞∞∞∞∞∞∞∞∞∞∞∞∞∞

I am grateful for...

_____
_____
_____
_____

Today I'm proud that I...

_____
_____
_____

How do you feel today?:

- ☐ Happy
- ☐ Sad
- ☐ Stressed
- ☐ Energized
- ☐ Tired
- ☐ Stressed
- ☐ Fearful
- ☐ Angry

- ☐ Peaceful
- ☐ Disappointed
- ☐ Anxious
- ☐ Annoyed
- ☐ Hopeful
- ☐ Calm
- ☐ Productive
- ☐ Excited

- ☐ Negative
- ☐ Strong
- ☐ Inspired
- ☐ Thankful
- ☐ Loving
- ☐ Loved
- ☐ _____
- ☐ _____

_____
_____

If this was your last moment on earth, what would you appreciate about it?

_____
_____
_____
_____
_____
_____
_____

DAILY
Gratitude

DATE : _____ _____ _____

I am grateful for...
_____
_____
_____
_____

What are you taking for granted about your day to day that you could be thankful for?
_____
_____
_____
_____
_____
_____

How do you feel today?:

- ☐ Happy
- ☐ Sad
- ☐ Stressed
- ☐ Energized
- ☐ Tired
- ☐ Stressed
- ☐ Fearful
- ☐ Angry

- ☐ Peaceful
- ☐ Disappointed
- ☐ Anxious
- ☐ Annoyed
- ☐ Hopeful
- ☐ Calm
- ☐ Productive
- ☐ Excited

- ☐ Negative
- ☐ Strong
- ☐ Inspired
- ☐ Thankful
- ☐ Loving
- ☐ Loved
- ☐ _____
- ☐ _____

_____
_____

⊙ Take Action: Reward effort, if someone does something nice for you, do something nice for them.

☐ Task Completed

DAILY
Gratitude

DATE : ____ ____ ____

◇◇

I am grateful for...

_____
_____
_____
_____

Positive Affirmation: I am...

_____
_____
_____

How do you feel today?:

- ☐ Happy
- ☐ Sad
- ☐ Stressed
- ☐ Energized
- ☐ Tired
- ☐ Stressed
- ☐ Fearful
- ☐ Angry

- ☐ Peaceful
- ☐ Disappointed
- ☐ Anxious
- ☐ Annoyed
- ☐ Hopeful
- ☐ Calm
- ☐ Productive
- ☐ Excited

- ☐ Negative
- ☐ Strong
- ☐ Inspired
- ☐ Thankful
- ☐ Loving
- ☐ Loved
- ☐ _____
- ☐ _____

_____
_____

Name three days in your life that you feel especially grateful for.

_____
_____
_____
_____
_____
_____
_____

DAILY
Gratitude

DATE : ____ ____ ____

◇◇◇

I am grateful for...
_____
_____
_____
_____

What vacation are you most grateful for?
_____
_____
_____
_____
_____

How do you feel today?:

- ☐ Happy
- ☐ Sad
- ☐ Stressed
- ☐ Energized
- ☐ Tired
- ☐ Stressed
- ☐ Fearful
- ☐ Angry

- ☐ Peaceful
- ☐ Disappointed
- ☐ Anxious
- ☐ Annoyed
- ☐ Hopeful
- ☐ Calm
- ☐ Productive
- ☐ Excited

- ☐ Negative
- ☐ Strong
- ☐ Inspired
- ☐ Thankful
- ☐ Loving
- ☐ Loved
- ☐ _____
- ☐ _____

I could have made today better by:
_____
_____
_____
_____

DAILY
Gratitude

DATE : _____ _____ _____

"You can start with nothing and still succeed. However, if you don't start you will never succeed." — Oscar Bimpong

I am grateful for...
_____
_____
_____

What's one thoughtful thing someone did for you recently?
_____
_____
_____
_____

How do you feel today?:

- ☐ Happy
- ☐ Sad
- ☐ Stressed
- ☐ Energized
- ☐ Tired
- ☐ Stressed
- ☐ Fearful
- ☐ Angry

- ☐ Peaceful
- ☐ Disappointed
- ☐ Anxious
- ☐ Annoyed
- ☐ Hopeful
- ☐ Calm
- ☐ Productive
- ☐ Excited

- ☐ Negative
- ☐ Strong
- ☐ Inspired
- ☐ Thankful
- ☐ Loving
- ☐ Loved
- ☐ _____
- ☐ _____

_____
_____

What abilities do I have that I'm grateful for?
_____
_____
_____
_____
_____

DAILY
Gratitude

DATE : ____ ____ ____

I am grateful for...

What is there about the challenges/difficulties I have experienced (or am currently experiencing) that I can be thankful for?

What is different today than it was a year ago that I'm thankful for?

DAILY
Gratitude

DATE : ____ ____ ____

"When you are grateful, fear disappears and abundance appears."
— Anthony Robbins

I am grateful for...
_____
_____
_____

How did I feel appreciated today?
_____
_____
_____
_____

How do you feel today?:

- ☐ Happy
- ☐ Sad
- ☐ Stressed
- ☐ Energized
- ☐ Tired
- ☐ Stressed
- ☐ Fearful
- ☐ Angry

- ☐ Peaceful
- ☐ Disappointed
- ☐ Anxious
- ☐ Annoyed
- ☐ Hopeful
- ☐ Calm
- ☐ Productive
- ☐ Excited

- ☐ Negative
- ☐ Strong
- ☐ Inspired
- ☐ Thankful
- ☐ Loving
- ☐ Loved
- ☐ _____
- ☐ _____

_____
_____

What positive habits did I engage in today?
_____
_____
_____
_____
_____
_____

www.ingramcontent.com/pod-product-compliance
Lightning Source LLC
Chambersburg PA
CBHW070936160426
43193CB00011B/1701